The Tin
Blue
Line

Jim Stone

authorHOUSE®

AuthorHouse™
1663 Liberty Drive
Bloomington, IN 47403
www.authorhouse.com
Phone: 1 (800) 839-8640

Published by AuthorHouse 08/20/2018

ISBN: 978-1-5462-2227-9 (sc)
ISBN: 978-1-5462-2226-2 (e)

Print information available on the last page.

CONTENTS

1

WHAT IS A POLICE OFFICER?

What is a police officer? This is a question I often ask myself. I am over a forty-year veteran of police work. I should know the answer to this question. I know the old stated purpose of a police officer, is the duty to protect and serve. But police work is far more than this duty. In fact, the answers are infinite.

I know that they wear many different hats. They encompass many different professions, and provide many public duties, from traffic directing to crime investigation. I know for sure that they are unbelievable human beings. They are human, but not infallible, as you will learn in this book.

A police officer has a combination or traits of what all humans are. A little mixture from anything from saint to sinner. A dust creation to a deity. Maybe in the angelic realm. Now comes all the descriptive adjectives and phrases. They are exceptional people; they are unusual; they are not common place to the human race. As stated above, they wear many different hats. Under that hat; in that blue uniform, and behind that badge, is a creature that is in a group; that less than one half of one percent misfit the uniform, or tarnish that badge.

That is better statistics than most professions including politicians, up to president and the clergy. You don't have to be crazy to work here, but it helps.

They are dedicated, proud individuals with big egos that like to complain, and bitch a lot. They are mostly stressed and unhappy about something. Because they of all people are the most needed, most demanded, most judged, most criticized. But they are expected to respond to any and all situations immediately, or there will be a slow response time complaint. I like to refer to the police as the most profiled, labeled, stereotyped, despised profession, even over dentist. Speaking of doctor, my doctor told me that his job as a doctor, he felt close to God, and that God worked through his hands. He said that now he believes that God works hand in hand and through police officers. I told him," me too and God is everywhere."

But a strange nameless human in uniform known only as the po-lice is usually, but not always referred to as sir to his face, and pig or worse to his back. When we were called pig, we said yes we are, because pig stands for pride, integrity, and guts. A lot of times false information, facts, and action are given on this public servant. Accusations are made before all the facts, investigation, evidence, witnesses are heard? Public opinion has taken over. I know that a police officer's laundry hangs out every day, on duty or not for viewing of the public and administration. And a lot of these viewers are looking for dirty laundry. It is really a love-hate situation.

The police officer must be a calm diplomat that can settle any situation, disputes between individuals in a way that each side feels that they won. Also keeps supervisors and department administrators happy. If a police officer is neat, clean, haircut, not one hair out of place, confident and professional, he is regarded as a good department image. But sometimes to some in the public, he may be considered to be conceited, labeled with preconceived opinions described with the standard terms.

He thinks he is all that. he is a tough guy. Thinks he is a bad ass, a bully using his authority to intimidate. He ain't shit without that gun and badge, lot of attitude, full of shit, a dick with ears, badge heavy. But if the officer is unkept due to intentional causes, or maybe the result of his last call or string of calls or maybe an altercation that may contribute to his appearance, mood, attitude and tone. But the unknowing public may label him a bum. One preconceived opinion is he probably just left the doughnut shop. Where he was talking, eating doughnuts and drinking coffee. That's all they do is eat, drive around drinking coffee. But like I said before if the officer is squared away, well kept, neat and clean, pleasant and friendly, but blunt and professional, they are a show-off, forward or a flirt. Professional, blunt business like he is a grouch or asshole.I don't like him. Irrespective of the thought, feelings, opinions, insults; the officer has to remain calm, rational but authoritative. Make instant fair decisions, use good judgement and handle the situation, no matter what is required.

This is why I say that these brave, dedicated men and women in blue should not have to bear another burden, to add to their stress from present duties. The threats of resistance, attack, serious injury or killed intentionally. The protest chants don't help. Pigs in a blanket, fry'em like bacon. What do we want? Dead cops, when do we want it? Now. The attacks and officers killed is increasing in stats.

But what if it was vice-versa. What if the police started calling for shooting violent criminals, drug dealers, thieves, robbers, and killers? Say fry'em like bacon, execute, death penalty. What do we want? Dead criminals. When do we want it? Now. Why? Save the government incarceration cost. Protect the community. Electrocution now. Look at the situation in Chicago, out of control. But then we would be a police state; a war. But we are already in war with factions.

That's why I refer to these brave men and women in blue, wearing what in the old west days was called a Tin Star, to maintain law and order, and keep the peace. Modern day, thus the tin blue line that remains calm and resolute in fighting back chaos, crime and anarchy. But it is a very thin tin blue line that sustains, maintains law and order, right and wrong, good and evil. I would hate to see a society without the tin blue line.

Another factor, is we used to work under the pressure of will the politicians, government and our own department support us in doing our sworn oath, doing our job. Will they have our back. I think we may have turned the corner in law and order, with this new Washington administration. I think law enforcement will receive the recognition and support they deserve, a new feeling of support, and that the police will have someone watching their back, besides it is realized that it is absolutely essential and needed.

Another important element of the Criminal Justice System. The officer is the key witness from the arrest, preliminary hearing to trial by judge or jury. It is a gamble, it can be dismissed, not prosecuted, probation, time sentence, found not guilty. But you have to attend probable cause hearing, arraignment, motions, resets, trial jury or judge. All court appearance is in addition to working your regular shift. This is time consuming and makes for a long day. You feel like you are on trial.

So, you can see that the police officer is a composite of several different professions, patrol officer, counselor, CSI tech, computer operator, constitutional expert, lawyer, district attorney, social worker, minister, drugs, defense expert, gun expert, marksman, MMA fighter, self-defense expert, mechanic, accident investigator, traffic and crowd control, special events and assignments, first aid and more inclusions, whatever the public demands. I do know that once you think you have seen about everything possible, something tops it.

But now on top of all these duties, and probably working 24-7 with moonlight jobs, regular shift and court time. He must provide a living for himself and his family on a very low pay. So he becomes an accountant, budget director, and CEO at home.

But police officers perform heroic actions every day which are just taken for granted as part of the job. This is done without any Thank You, or notoriety or recognition. But none is asked for. It's my job, I do my job. It is amazing how many crimes are solved, how many criminals took off the street, how many people are helped, how many lives are saved. How many calls are handled- problems solved every day.

Have copies and documentation of everything you do. Maintain a good chain of evidence. The least hands involved in it the better. This is important when dealing with your peers, administration, courthouse and any time in the future to explain this case to anyone, they are quick to criticize the quality of the investigation, charges, case and how it was handled. And of course you are going to be accused of dishonesty, false testimony, questionable evidence. Also not remembering the accurate facts and evidence of the case. That you are a poor officer or investigator. Also files disappear for one reason or the other. You can do a good job on a hundred different cases, with good arrest, but you will be remembered and talked about for any questionable case or investigation. Don't screw up on anything because you will never live the story down. In fact the screw-up cases, evidence and investigations are used as a training tool as to what not to do. I even used it. There is also a lot of jealousy involved with all the big egos you work with. But that is police work. But you learn by experience.

Of course the police officer has to be the first to arrive at the scene of an automobile accident or as we called them vehicles, which cover everything. Must immediately check for death or injury, commence first aid, start breathing, stop bleeding, treat for shock, identify drivers, passengers and position. Tie splints to injured limbs, treat head concussion and insure that all receive medical treatment or hospital emergency care, that all leave the scene as healthy as possible, even if they say they are O.K. Determine what happened, collect all evidence, witnesses statements, make reports, traffic report diagram, pictures, etc. If it is a fatality or more than one the investigation continues. It becomes a crime scene; where the whole crime scene is measured, photos of skid marks, debris, and follow-up at hospital and morgue. Next of kin notified and also the media, then filing appropriate charges and a court date.

The police officer must have knowledge of guns and knives and anything that can be used as a weapon, offensive weapon or a dangerous weapon or object that can be used as a weapon. No matter how visible or concealed. The officer must be aware and developes knowledge and instinct to spot these weapons, and where they are concealed and be aware of any sudden movement. A general pat down for weapons as a safety factor is a good idea.

Sometimes it becomes necessary to use deadly force to protect yourself or a third person. Your last resort, final option. Sometimes it happens fast and you have to respond in seconds. Unfortunately, you cannot pick the situation, time, location, scenario, light or darkness, weather, close combat, a fight or struggle in a life or death situation. It may be on the run. If an officer is in one of these situations, and he does have too shoot, it must be somewhere where it doesn't hurt. And protect the perpetrator from injury or being killed. The officer must be able to combat one or more criminals twice his size, and probably half his age. Especially older officers with their gas, baton, fist or feet. But they have to do it in a way that don't injure them. Police brutality, defending yourself and life. Also remember to not damage your uniform. Now days the officers have instant communication, video and audio, stun guns, and tasers. Back in the day we did not have this equipment, the closest radio to call for back-up or help was in the car. You was on your own. Now they even have car cameras and body cams. A lot of this is good and bad. You will respond with how you were trained, but in life or death situation you may respond with whatever it takes to survive. The survival instinct story. If a police officer lets someone abuse him or hit him or put hands on him or her and don't respond, he is a coward. If the officer responds with a demand for compliance by putting hands on the criminal, touches, or moves him around, hits, they are guilty of police brutality. We used to have a saying that when in conversation with an individual you don't touch me, I won't touch you.

I remember one incident where an officer was involved in a foot chase and struggle . The officer was shot and killed by the perpetrator. The question here is when help arrived, he was located and had his taser gun in his hand. Service weapon in the holster? Being politically correct and even politics is creeping more into law enforcement more than ever before. In my opinion they are two completely different things.

Now days I hear all these stories that the police are out to brutalize and kill intentionally. In fact the people

I worked with, this was the last thing and wish on our list. Our wish list consisted of a wish for quite, low calls, drama free, trouble free. A shift with no altercations, no violence. No use of necessary force, no force of any kind. No one injured, no one killed, especially us. Then after a nice quite shift we could go home alive to family uninjured. But of course this was a wish list. We see, and deal with the dark, dirty part of society mostly deal with crime, troubled people, drugs, alcohol part of society, and mentally challenged, and people on drug highs, gangs, and teens. We don't profile, this is just the segment of society we have to work with. It is amazing as I write this story there was a breaking news story on T.V that is similar to what I am writing about. Traffic accidents, being safe, alert, observant, looking for weapons. Like I wrote: before police officers have to wear many different hats. One mistake could be your last. It may be fate, but it is truly a message. I like Murphy's Laws, if anything can go wrong, anything will go wrong. News Report;

An officer received and responded to a one vehicle accident, where the vehicle sustained heavy damage. Two people trapped inside the vehicle. I believe they said the officer had served six years with the department. He had a nickname of Teddy Bear. This caught my ear also, because some citizens called me Teddy Bear on the streets and businesses in town. This officer evidently went out of police mode, into medic mode helper trying to get the trapped people out. Save lives and summon rescue, and medical help. And a traffic accident investigation. Unfortunately, one or both of the occupants trapped in the vehicle, shot and killed the officer. The officer had fourteen gunshot wounds. Fatal. Rest in peace my brother, Teddy Bear; I yearn for the day we not only rest in peace, we can also live in peace too, thank you for your service and sacrifice. Thanks for your dedication to duty. You died helping others and trying to do the right things.

The instant decisions that officers make, course of action that an officer takes will later have to be proved correct. The judgement, actions, arrest and charges, witnesses, evidence, photos, diagram, use of force, procedures, laws, constitutional rights will be highly dissected and scrutinized by the department, district attorney, lawyers and judges, it could take days, even months to render a decision on how to proceed with charges and trial. In felony cases the Grand Jury has to true bill the indictment.

If the officer made snap decisions, hurried his investigation he could be labeled careless, and maybe a bad case and incompetent in police work. Did not build a good concise evidence plus facts case. In other words, you have to have your ducks in a row. The most prepared wins. There is a lot of factors that compromise the case or crime scene evidence. Maybe the facts create reasonable doubt for the defense lawyer. Inadmissible evidence, search and seizure or confessions or statements questionable.

But on the other hand if the officer is deliberate, spends some time on the case investigation, working in a professional chronological order of doting all the I's, and crossing all the T's. Then he could be labeled as obstructing, slow, a false accusation. No evidence, poor investigator. Besides the heat is always on to clear reports and make arrests. Believe me there is a lot of peer pressure. Always watching and listening, they may steal the case right out from under you. Just too look good. That is why CYA is so important. Cover your ass!

The police officer from the start is expected to find evidence that describes either the weapon or criminal(s) and from this minute piece of evidence such as hair, bloodstain, print, track, semen, and from this describe the criminal, identify the criminal, his mode of operation, his weapon and who it is and where he is hiding? Then go make an arrest, clear the case. But now if you do great work, great investigation, with an arrest. You may hear, well he is just lucky.

If you don't catch the criminal; the case drags on, no new developments, no leads, no arrest. Then you may be labeled as not doing your job, lazy, poor investigator or incompetent. The officer has a crime scene, may or may not have witnesses, so he runs files, contacts victims and witnesses searching for leads. Take statements, logs, evidence, maintains a log. Look at files, other reports, mug shots, records, possible suspects and prints.

If the officer is able to connect with the perpetrator and him or her identified. Officer then has to file his reports, obtain an arrest warrant. Set a hearing in court to start the accusation, probable cause for the arrest and any evidence to appear at the Grand Jury if there is probable cause to bind it over. Sometimes your body and eyes will ache from all this investigating, viewing paper work, computer search. Hours and hours of surveillance spent. All in effort and satisfaction of getting a felon off the streets, clearing the case for yourself and the victims. The felon will probably get dealt out, plea bargain or by a shameless lawyer who finds a loophole or technicality or who he knows. But the lawyer will say that he was just defending his client, making sure he received all his rights and a fair trial. They usually leave the court room in a strut, pounding their victory chest, and laughing and high fiving. I wish the arrest and investigation was the end of the police job, but as you can see it is not, you enter another complex difficult stage prosecution and court stage.

Sometimes an officer in certain situations or circumstances has to take action under what is called exigent circumstances. This usually breaks away from standard operating procedures. It is used in emergency incidents, extreme, where inaction would be a miscarriage of Justice in case of severe injury, life or death, where time is of the essence, whatever the officer does in this circumstance, the officer is acting in a good faith effort.

Also, no matter what is going on in the media any police connected matters by any department anywhere administration, accusation or any police organization draws attention to all officers in uniform. But these officers keep showing up at work to do their job, cover their shift no matter what the circumstances are around them. But they know that they are under the eye, and stereotyped due to unsubstantiated information and accusations which usually turn out to be false.

Blessed are the peacemakers, for they shall be called children of God.

Matthews 5-9

Then the men and women in blue, and wearing a tin star badge are often referred to as peace officers. I do associate this with keeping the peace, peace and tranquility. There are Justice of the Peace. My favorite is peace of mind. Whatever happens remain calm, but ready to react, try not to get too stressed. Which brings up the subject of officers lost in the line of duty, like what happened today to Teddy Bear. RIP. Greater love hath no man than this he lay down his life for his friends John 15:13

Another thin line is the use of confidential informants. I had them, but I also had friends and concerned citizens who provided information, tips, and intelligence. A lot of them had provided true and reliable information in the past. Not like an informant who provides information in a fairly consistent manner, and beneficial tips. the information from friends and acquaintances were done in a free, unconditional manner without regard to a goal or reward. Just trying to help. But everyone wants to know who the source or informant is, officers, detectives, administration, lawyers, district attorney, judges. I have been asked in open court, threat of arrest, badgering by counsel, judges, and department members. Even if it meant losing the case, I would not give up the source or informant who provided the information.! I gave my word to protect them. I watched a story on T.V. news of a female reporter in Washington D.C. was jailed for months, but would not give up her source.

I had an incident happen where a drug detective told a politician the name of an informant in a pretty big drug case. I wasn't involved. A short time later this same informant was found dead in a sleazy motel room with a huge amount of cocaine, in a clear plastic baggy shoved down his throat. Not on my watch. Loose lips sinks ships.

I always say I never done everything right, but I didn't do anything wrong. A clear conscious no benefits. Actually worked too hard. Never stabbed anyone in the back, or sailed anyone down the river. But it is said, it is better to give than to receive. That's why I try to write the light hearted and humorous side of the job.

There was also a thin line on investigations of cases, the rumors, and suspicions started to circulate. No conclusion or further information if it was slow; no arrest, proper paperwork filed late, drag on the case, there was~ jealousy, suspicion. You may be corrupt, and maybe covering for someone, and maybe you should be investigated, especially in drug cases.

Then if you started making a lot of arrest, confiscating a lot of drugs and money. Putting drug dealers in jail. Flip the coin, where is he getting information, stepping on toes, friends of friends, helping notable figures and consorting with the underworld. No thoughts to the fact that you are working, investigating, gathering information from trusted sources, who put their faith and confidence in the officer try to help. But a lot of your peers can't believe what good police work will do.

I even heard that," Well he better not mess with any of my friends." You can be framed and set-up. Informants flip. He has got to be on the take, covering for others, corrupt and needs to be investigated. I have been all this. It really hurts your feelings after so much hard work. Too be accused. He can't be that good but good results come from foot pounding the pavement, looking, observing, beating the bushes. A rapport with people who want to help, and make a difference, especially drug investigations which I believe leads to not all crime, but a great portion. I think working drugs, you have your finger on the problem. Old school police tactics.

So you see this job is a piece of cake, no problem. But wait now add hundreds of new cases and incidents, x 365 days, x years of service.

2

Man Eating a Doughnut

While writing the story about preconceived notions that police officers stay in the doughnut shop eating doughnuts, this reminded me of a beat partner of mine. He worked an adjacent beat to mine and was sort of the clown of the watch. He spent a lot of time at the doughnut shop. (1) He liked coffee and (2) It was about the only thing open on the Graveyard Shift (11pm to 7am). And the employees always loved the officers to come by, it made them feel safe at night. I will call this officer BM. BM was a veteran of several years. BM was small in stature, 160lbs or so, under 6', skinny, with a large nose, receding hair line, with a leather textured skin. His speech was real country, a country drawl, and spoke in phrases. He had a good attitude, and was really funny especially with some of his radio transmissions, which were many.

One morning, early hours, I was patrolling when BM come on the radio with that slow country drawl.

6-oh-6

Radio: 606. Go ahead.

6-oh-6: A man eatin a doughnut said there is a vehicle wreck at Waswell Road and 285.

Radio: 606 Ok. You in route?

Yep!

One of a kind, BM.

3

HAWAII (CAN YOU HEAR ME NOW?)

Again on the Graveyard Shift, BM was working 606. I guess about 0300 hours radio dispatch started calling 6-0-6. There was no answer.

6-0-6?

6-0-6?

6-0-6?

Alarms went off in everybody's head. Concerned I checked the doughnut shop first, looking for BM. There was a safety and welfare concern. Radio did not have him logged out at any location. After some time radio kept trying to raise 6-0-6. They did a signal emergency beep.

Radio: calling 6-0-6?

6-0-6

6-oh-6

Radio: Radio has been trying to raise you! Do you copy, how do you copy?

6-oh-6 You sound purty good, but it sounds like you're n Hawaii or som-um. He was given a signal to go to the precinct for information, and get his radio checked. I guess he had a bad radio. But at least he was safe, and not in peril.

4

WALKIN' THE DOG

One more BM story. A few years ago, someone manufactured a stiff dog leash. It indicated a dog on a leash, but the dog was imaginary. Invisible novelty joke. A lot of them were sold. Again on the graveyard shift around 0430 hours (430 am).

6-oh-6"

Radio: Go ahead 606

6-0-6 Hold me out on Copeland Road with a man walkin' a dog and ain't got no dog.

Radio: K

5

Do You Know Jesus?

I worked with a shift sergeant on the graveyard shift. Sarge was of Russian descent, or at least from part of the old Soviet Union (Lithawania). He then worked his way to Ireland, where he spent several years. This is how a unique and unusual speech dialect and tone was created and developed. Sarge's voice was very stern and intimidating. A mixture of Russian, German, and Irish. Along with his speech was a large specimen of a man: tall, broad shoulders, 200 lbs. plus, a large, towering frame. A rugged texture of skin with large ears and nose. He reminded me of the German Nazis, or the German Gestapo, especially with his neat fitting uniform. This is how he projected. Anyway, Sarge finally made it into the U.S.

One day as we were having lunch, Sarge started telling me stories. He was relating some of his life history, stories about his mom and dad.

"You know, Jimmy, l'ma half a Jew?"

"Really? Which half?"

Shitbird. Then he discussed World War II. How he and his family made it to Ireland, and then to the U.S. He told me that he served in the army. I asked as a joke,

"Which side did you fight for?"

He had a good sense of humor, takes jokes as well. He replied with some colorful language, saying it only how Sarge could say it, smart ass. Like I said, he could take a joke, good guy, great dependable partner and friend. I loved him like a brother. Really I could write a book about the Sarge character and all his stories. He was a joy to work with, and was a good dependable beat partner, and back-up partner. He also had your back as shift sergeant. He was the source of many war stories. There was nothing like telling and sharing stories. Due to this and conversations and insults and opinions, officers had to have a leather-tough skin, not sensitive thin skin. I did notice Sarge's arm had the German J.D. number.

One story I recall occurred on a cold wintery night, or morning. I should say, since it was about 0400 hrs. It was maybe December or January. Early morning hours on the graveyard shift, called the morning watch. We were referred to as the A-team for the job this watch did solving crimes, catching criminals, enforcing the law. Pro-active and productive statistics.

Anyway, one of the morning watch officers pulled over in the grass on the freeway to observe traffic and maybe catch a violator or drunk driver. Evidently, this officer got warm and cozy, relaxed and comfortable, and soon dozed off. He had left his car running with all of the lights on, and parked on the side of the freeway. Sarge came patrolling along and spots the car parked, lights on, creating a little concern. So Sarge pulls up behind the car, observes for a few seconds: no response.

Sarge toots his horn, he hits the blue lights, and then the siren; no response to any of these actions. So Sarge gets out of his car and walks cautiously up to the car., driver side door window. He observed the officer's mouth was gaped open, maybe drooling. Sarge shines his flashlight inside the car, still no response. So he taps on the door glass with his maglight. The officer was startled, shocked, and disoriented. He started rolling down his window. Looking up at a large police sergeant, also his supervisor, he blurted out,

"Jesus Christ!!"

In that stern German Gestapo voice with a gruff foreign accent,

"NO, IT'S NOT JESUS CHRIST, IT'S YOUR SERGEANT! WHAT ARE YOU DOING ASLEEP, LAD?"

Maybe the officer was thinking about the Hispanic wrecker driver, Jesus?

Fill in Quotes

S ometimes stumbling blocks can become stepping stones

It is better to have it and not need it.
Than to need it and not have it.

Always know your exact location at all times.
It's hard to get help if they don't know where you are at

If anything can go wrong, it will go wrong.

Expect the unexpected.

The best prepared will win.

Be honest and true too your word.

Do not tarnish the badge

We are the Thin Blue Line between good and evil.

Don't misfit the uniform, remember we must maintain the trust, we are the main line of defense.

6

Howling at the Moon in the Wrong Pants

Oh good. About 0400 hrs. on the graveyard shift, about to get another shift made, only three more hours, maybe, if I don't get tied up on a late call. But I am not usually that lucky. It's always an early morning incident or traffic accident in all the early morning traffic and gridlock. It's kind of slow right now, but circumstances can change in the blink of an eye. I've heard it said that this job is 98% boredom and 2% holy terror, especially on this shift. I've had my share of boring, long nights and then butt-puckering incidents. But what's the old saying? You ask for it and somebody has got to do it. Most all the businesses are closed so it is a constant patrol of the businesses, front and back, looking for burglars. Same thing with subdivisions and apartments, looking for suspicious people, thieves, and burglars on foot, vehicles, motorcycles, and bikes, operating at night when it's dark, and most people are sleeping. Lots of opportunity, and all the accidents and calls for service. It is also a full moon tonight. The crazies come out on a full moon. It seems like when there is a full moon, just weird things happen.

Radio dispatch.

"136?"

"136."

"2880 Holsom Bridge Rd., signal28, possible 38-D. Be a white male, early 20's long brown hair, flowered colored shirt, jeans laying in front of the business, howling at the moon."

"2880 Holsom Bridge Rd., 28, howling. Ok."

This signal is an intoxicated person, possibly using alcohol and drugs. This location is a Mexican sports bar, with a lot of mural paintings, especially of Mexican boxers. Cesar Chaves is very popular. I don't get a lot of calls there. I know the owner, he is a nice guy.

136-26 (on the scene): Okay, well at least he is not hard to find. Caucasian male, early 20s, with long, brown hair, multi-colored shirt, jeans, and sandals laying on his back on one of the outside cement tables. Gazing into the sky doing his best imitation of a wolf howling in the moonlight.

"Ah-woo!! Ah-woooo, woooo!!"

I'm going to observe him for a minute, because he is oblivious to my presence and his. I don't see any signs of an injury, and no signs or visibility of any weapons. It appears that he is alone. The wolf "wooo" is continuing. This must be the guy. I guess I will get out and see what's going on.

"Hey. hello, sir. Are you alright?"

The guy is somewhat surprised: "Yeah."

"Well, ok. Why don't you stand up here and talk to me for a minute?"

Ooops. That might have been the wrong instruction because he is extremely unsteady on his feet, wobbly and I had to catch him and hold him up. The last thing I want is for him to fall and injure himself, requiring an ambulance and trip to the hospital.

"Well sir, just sit down on this table seat for now, ok."

I guided him to the seat, maintaining his balance.

"Well sir, why are you laying out here on a table, howling at the moon?"

"Well, it's a full moon."

"You have a strong odor of alcoholic beverage on your breath and person. You been drinking quite a bit tonight?"

"Yeah, I had a couple of beers." He slurred out.

This guy is really out of it, intoxicated, doesn't know where he is or what he's doing. He does not have a clue.

"Sir, do you have a driver's license or some form of ID?"

Slurred: "No, I don't have any license."

"Anything with your name on it?"

"Nah."

"What is your name? And how old are you?"

He finally provided me with a name and a date of birth. I am not sure how accurate it is. But I did check for wants and wanted. No wants under this information or date of birth, but I am not sure who he is. Now he cannot provide me with a good address or any family information or phone number. Nobody to call to come pick him up, no money for a taxi and he sure can't walk home. So I went through all the questions with him.

"Where do you live?"

"I don't really know."

"Is it close by?"

"I think it's about 2 miles."

"So you still live at home with family?"

"No. I just moved. Maybe it's about 5 miles."

"Is there a family member I can call?"

"Nah, no family here. I'm in an apartment."

"OK. Where?"

"I got a roommate."

"What's his name?"

"I can't remember."

"So do you have a phone number for him?"

"Nah I don't he won't answer the phone anyway. I just moved in with him."

Ok, it appears I am getting nowhere fast. Actually, this guy has become more intoxicated and very unstable mentally and physically. He really needs a drying out period somewhere safe, maybe county jail.

"Ok sir. Stand up I need to check you more closely for any weapons."

As I was checking this guy for weapons he had a large bulge in his right front pocket. It was a clear plastic sandwich bag containing a green leafy material that looked, smelled, and that I recognized as marijuana. Suspected marijuana.

"Sir, you are under arrest for public drunkenness and possession of marijuana, maybe more than an ounce. Under the state violation, controlled substance act."

I advised him of his rights.

"That's not my marijuana!"

"It was in your pants pocket."

"Yeah but these ain't my pants?"

Ok, on to county jail. Nice, funny guy just too much alcohol and chemicals. But it did put a smile on my face. I think I've heard about every excuse now. The lessons learned: don't drink and smoke on a full moon. If you do, have a ride home. Don't wolf call "ah-woo" at the moon, and for sure wear your own pants. And make sure they are not pants on fire. Remember that possession is probably 98-99% of the law.

7

30-W (WHO, WHAT WHEN, WHERE)

One of the main things emphasized and dwelled upon in police work was proper radio procedures. The utilization of good communication procedures and skills that follow the rules and regulations and a standard operating procedure. In other words, don't play on the radio, no sly opinion remarks, snickers, whistles, or cat calls and so forth. Don't comment on the officers transmissions or calls. Don't click the mic or whisper or snicker at comments. But, yet it was a common occurrence. It was also pretty common for a microphone to get stuck, or get the mic button stuck by sitting on it, or laying them down, maybe in the seat. You could hear some funny conversations, comments. But also some serious comments are transmitted. Then there was the fact these comments, transmissions and actions were open to a lot or ears, even to the media.

This really changed over the years with a more sophisticated system, better training. Now due to safety of the officers, you can push the mic button, they know who it is, identifies. Now there is even body and auto cams. But the stuck mic still continues. When this happens the whole conversion and sounds goes over the air to a lot of ears. This can be quite hilarious, but can be somewhat self-incriminating. It could be derogatory, insulting or complaints about the job. It could involve the administration, other officers or supervisors, prisoners or call information. I remember one time back in the day and everyone's ears perked open, full attention to the radio transmission. What? listen to this shit. I can't remember the whole conversation verbatim but it went sorta like this: It was scratchy and muffled. You had to lean in and listen carefully, a lot of break-ups.

You heard a rustling sound involving the microphone button, and you can hear that the mic button is stuck. I think you hear it a lot nowadays, called a "Hot Mic." Oops! You could hear the car doors open and then shut. Then you hear a muffled male voice and then a female voice. Then more rustling sounds and some kissy sounds, then silence. Anticipation is growing. Hi, honey, are you ready for me? Hey, baby. You know I am. I can't wait, where you want to do it? Right here on the front seat, spread it out right here whoa! I got to hear this. Breaking up, some inaudible. Who is that? More rustling in the seat. Oh that feels good. You want a drink? Yes, why not. I brought some stuff to put on it, take all that off. I like those big breasts, and those fat little thighs. You like them. Oh yes, you want a piece. Yeah I want a piece looks and smells good. I want to taste that while its hot and juicy um that's good, taste it. Put your tongue on it. O.K. put it in here, you want me to take it out for you. Yeah, unzip this, look how pink and hard it is, then later, wait can you get all that in your mouth. I'm choking its too big. Here let me give you half only. Oh grab it. You're not going to eat that nasty thing now are you? That looks like mayonnaise, plus more conversation, but this was the gist of the conversation. Now, what do you think was going on? Don't make a judgement, let all the facts and evidence come out, then form a conclusion.

What actually happened here, or the rest of the story, the real story. An officer's wife met him for lunch, with intentions of sharing a picnic lunch with her husband. She wanted to do something special for him, so she brought a picnic basket filled with chicken, sandwich meat, lettuce and tomatoes, condiments, hot apple pies, drinks, chips and even some bubble gum. She brought a table cloth to spread out and a pillow to put behind his back. She had the sandwich stuff wrapped in a zip-lock bag. During the meeting she made a large sub sandwich with French bread loaded with meat, lettuce, tomato, condiments a lot of mayonnaise. But it was too big to eat it, almost choked her. She cut it in half to split with her husband, she laid her half on the seat, that got knocked off the seat. He saw it and said grab it, but it rolled onto the floorboard. Some of the mayonnaise was on the seat and on his pant leg. The officer decided to eat it anyway since it still had the paper around it. The wife thought the sandwich half went in the floor and was nasty. Careful on drawing conclusions.

O.K. back to the main story. Then you had people who just like to hang around the police, a police wannabe curious, groupie, self-appointed deputy, citizen patrol or helper. Maybe even a psychological problem, infatuation. We had a code for these people-24.

They get the feeling that they are actually a part of the department, imagination running wild. Some were quite serious, believable and knowledgeable in police work. A lot of them took on the look and demeanor of a trained police officer. So this type was hard to figure out and hard to be identified in a large department of many officers and personnel. Some were hard to catch on to right away. There were incidents where these individuals showed up on calls and incidents. Some had portable scanners.

One incident I recall that involved one of these demented people was because it was both serious, and humorous. And almost unbelievable. It occurred at the county hospital. A public hospital that served a million people from all over the state, and sometimes out of state. It was always extremely busy 24-7. We called it the meat market, like a war battle injury zone. Sick people, shot people, stab victims, accident victims, burn victims, homeless, amputee, drunks. You name it, it was there. It's funny how you adapt to these conditions and take them for granted. It sure lets you know that we are all just a number and not invincible. But being a County City Hospital it had a small holding cell unit for prisoners who needed treatment, blood tests, medical care, perps from jail. That little precinct was usually constantly busy. One thing was, just about everyone you arrested claimed to be injured or sick and needed to go to the hospital. So this little hospital holding facility was very busy with all the prisoners, plus drivers charged with driving under the influence were brought there for blood test. There was a lot of in and out foot traffic from officers and prisoners.

This one rookie officer, assigned to a downtown paddy wagon brought in several prisoners charged with a variety of charges. He had a handful of tickets. The sign-in officer was very busy with incoming prisoners and officers. In fact, it was crowded. A lot of prisoners being checked in. All of a sudden a small crowd had gathered, of prisoners, police officers and civilians that extended out into the hall from the Security Office. Everybody was shooting the shit, visiting while they waited. Grab-assing, telling war stories. In fact, there was several conversations going on at the same time. I thought it was chaos. All of a sudden the desk officer said he was handed some tickets (citations) but is missing a person in number. A prisoner is missing. One prisoner in all the commotion had escaped. There was a disagreement in whose custody the prisoner was in between the desk officer and paddy wagon driver. But we know now that we have had a prisoner to escape. We had to check all the tickets to prisoners to see who it is, and what he looks like, then put a lookout for him especially around the hospital.

It was quite chaotic and serious to let a prisoner escape custody. It is a bad no-no to let a prisoner escape, violation of rules and regulations and standard operating procedures. It is usually handled by disciplinary action. Then it was a bad reputation to have that you allowed a prisoner to escape. It questions your competency and is terrible peer pressure. In fact, one of the key ways to learn and gain experience was through mistakes of other officers. I sure finally started using every edge and information to do my job. Anyway to say the least it was chaos. Whose responsible, arguments, identify and place a lookout to see if we could recapture this prisoner.

During all this chaos the paddy wagon driver was trying to figure out his situation and what he should do.

All of a sudden a short fat guy I call him round dressed in a white style dress shirt and a bow tie with neatly combed hair, late twenties, who was trying to take charge from the wagon driver.

He said

Let me see your walkie-talkie.

The wagon driver handed him his radio.

What's your call number?

My what?

What's your radio number?

Unit?

Oh 30-W

The guy gets the radio.

30-W to base?

This is immediately recognized as not proper radio procedure. He keeps talking. Then officers begin to wonder who this guy is. Nobody knows him and he could not identify himself with a badge or ID. So the radio was wrestled away from him. The wagon driver said he didn't know the guy and he spoke so authoritative and efficient he thought he was a detective. He was just a demented police wannabe that I described earlier but it did add some humor to a bad situation. Police work, just when you think you have seen about everything then something happens that tops everything else. Not knowing then I would come in contact with more of these characters during my career, but I now had experience that they are around.

8

TAXI

My closest story to where there was a misidentification was vice-versa. I was parked on a side street in downtown in front of a hotel, which also had a bar. We had a lot of reported crimes in the area: prostitution, cars broken into, thefts. Some patrons had been robbed or rolled. So I just mingled in, and parked my patrol car in a regular parking space on the street, so not to be obvious and seen right away. A spot where I thought I would not be readily observed. I was sitting there observing, watching and looking for criminals, crimes, or suspicious activity. All of a sudden, here comes a guy staggering out of the hotel bar. He somewhat walked towards my car. this guy is short, heavy-set, big stomach. He was very unstable on his feet, walking with a lean forward, almost a run. I thought he was for sure gonna pitch forward and fall. He was probably mid-40s, sport coat, tie loose, shirt pulled out of his pants. Heavily intoxicated. I thought, " Man, this is a potential victim for sure." But instead he stumbles to my marked police car, opens the back door, actually flops down in the back seat with a thud. Slams the door. In a very slurred speech blurted out" Ey, take me to Fan and Bill's."

9

I'M MOVING

We had been having a lot of traffic accidents in a couple of areas. Some with statistics of serious injuries, and in some cases fatalities. All statistics and records were looked at. They provided statistics even from insurance companies. One stat that was mentioned was that statistics show that these serious accidents occur within two to five miles of your home. I was asked what my thoughts were. I said "Well I think I am going to move."

10

HOW TO STRIP A CAR

We had a large amount of crime, on what we called the Boulevard. Actually it was skid row. It was a variety of crimes 24/7. Everything: robbery, thefts, assaults, prostitution, drug use and sales, even murder. Full of bars, strip joints, motels. you name it, Even detectives and off-duty officers were cautious in covering their ass and their wallet. I come in one day a little late for shift change. Everybody was sitting around shooting the shit in the precinct office. There were officers getting off and coming on duty. They were curious. "Where you been? You get tied up on something?" I thought I would have a little fun. I said "Yeah, I was down on the Boulevard and I had a flat tire." So I pulled over on the side of the road, jacked my car up. I was taking the lug nuts off, to remove the wheel, and replace it with my spare. While I'm working doing that, this big black guy comes up, raises the hood, and with a wrench starts taking the battery loose to get it off. I said" Hey, what are you doing?", he said" It's alright man, you can have the tires and wheels, I just need the battery."

FILL IN QUOTES

Here is to all the people who get back up more times than they are knocked down. Who give more than they ever expect to receive. Who still show love to others even when their own heart is broken. Who smile through the sad times. Who fight the way for others? Who spread laughter and joy. Thank you for making the world a better place.

Never discredit your gut instinct. You are not paranoid. Your body can pick up on bad vibrations. If something deep inside of you says something is not right about a person or situation trust it.

11

SLIM JIM

I always tried to be humorous, and do light hearted police work when it was appropriate. A little bit of practical joking. Too many times, police officers are labeled to stern, grouch, no sense of humor, too serious. It's because everything you do and say is considered official to some people. But I did it anyway, when dealing with people. You can always change attitude and actions, graduate with the situation. I was patrolling one day, I drove through the large government parking lot of where our precinct was located, and other agency departments were located. I saw one of the fireman standing outside a vehicle parked in the employee parking. He was kind of looking around, a lost look. I assumed he was standing beside his personal vehicle. He flagged me down. I pulled my car up to him and got out. I said

"What happened? Did someone break in your car or did you lock your keys inside the car?"

"Yes, I'm locked out. Do you have a slim jim (device used to open car door locks)?"

I said, "Yes, I have one in the trunk. Do you want me to get it out, and we can see if we can get the door unlocked?"

He said, anxiously, and with a puzzled look, "Yes, thanks, that would be great. I feel stupid."

"Ok." I said, with a serious and solemn tone. I started opening the trunk.

"I also have the county issued slim jim, if you would prefer."

He was excited to hear this. "What is it? Is it like a slim jim?"

Calmly, I said, "Sorta like a slim jim. It's a big rock!"

12

Thin Line

Back in the day, I wrote about officers playing on the radio. Clicking, making little statements about other officers' calls or questions asked by the officer. Sometimes a call was hard to find, street numbers changed and jumped. Anyway, part of the city was in another county, and if you didn't know the area, it was confusing. A lot of times, it was a jurisdiction problem. One night, an officer was working the area.

"143."

"Go ahead 143."

"143. What separates the city and the Dekalb County line?"

Radio hesitated. Then, over the radio came a low voice, almost a whisper,

"A very thin line."

13

SURRENDER

Some things just happen. A famous term is shit happens. I know that when an officer came in and started his story. Listen to this shit. You ain't gonna believe this shit. This is a war story. There is also a saying you can't make this stuff up. One early morning about 0300 hours or so. I was parked beside my beat partner driver window to driver window. We were discussing how we just handled a previous call. We were parked in a lot of an open service gas station. Across one street, there on the other corner, was a restaurant bar called the Lark and Dove. Suddenly I see a tan four door Oldsmobile turn left into the service station off the main five lane road. Trouble is he missed the drive way, drove over a high curb; started bouncing like a yo-yo. I felt sure there was damage, especially under carriage. It sure was loud but he made it into the lot, pulled right up in front of us. Rolls down the driver's window glass. It's a male traveling alone, appeared to have been indulging in alcoholic beverages for awhile. The normal, the hair in disarray like he just woke up, red eyes like he just got out of bed, suit coat, white shirt with his tie loose, slouched in the seat. He was heavy set, 240lbs and 50 years old. Very slurred speech, how I know this is how he spoke. Scuse may ocifers, can you tell me where's a place called the Laurk and Love.

14

CONTACTS

This rookie officer was just out on solo patrol for the first time. He observes a vehicle travel slowly through a stop sign. No Stop. The old rolling stop. A traffic case. Time to do my job,to enforce the law,protect and serve. This is how crime starts. He blue lights and taps the siren. The vehicle stops,the officer gets out,and walks to the drivers door. The vehicle is being operated by a young female driver. Drivers license and proof of insurance Ma'am. Why are you stopping me? The reason I pulled you over is you failed to come to a complete stop at the stop sign back there. I stopped. Then the officer then says,I will be right back,because in his training he was taught to check the tag and driver's license for stolen,wants,warrants and wanted on the computer N.C.I.C.,G.C.I.C. Anyway,no wants,so he goes back up to the driver. Ok your license says that you are supposed to be wearing glasses. Look officer I have contacts you know. Look lady you violated the law, and I don't care who you know.

15

Sick?

The facts are that every job in America is politically partisan, buddy system, who you know, who knows you, one click after another, power and authority, political, P.C. and friends with benefits. Ratio and so on. That is a whole different story. So, there are promotions, appointments, decision and assignments based on these factors, whatever is politically correct. The old nose up the ass. The yes factor, a lot of butt kissing. It does leave a bad taste and the eyes roll; It is a time of silence and head shakes. Let the bitching begin, when it happens. All you can do is suck it up, except it, come in and do your best to be a good police officer and do your job. Separate the two. I guess this is when you don't make waves, turn the apple cart over. You are loyal and become a company person. Doing your job, working hard, fighting crime is the last factor considered. In fact you do such a good job they keep you an Indian. I know I was a training officer for years, so long that I wound up working for some of my trainees? But I had a job? Anyway one of my favorite true stories, out of many, illustrates all of the above and is sort of poetic justice. How the truth finally comes out in reality. There was a promotion made to Detective. Eyes rolled, heads shook, rumors started through the grapevine. Then it was announced that he would be working homicide? Wow! Eye rolls and shaking heads were at an all-time high. This job requires a good detective that can handle a critical crime scene investigation. That deer in the headlights look on everybody's face. Even nervous laughs. What? Why? Who? When? How? Where? Then later there was a critical shooting, and the victim was transported to the county hospital to try to save his life. A definite life and death situation. This was commonly referred too, that the victim was critical and low sick. The odds of survival were slim and none. Probably would be unable to hear what happen. Who did it, and maybe a dying declaration. It may be only none, slim had already left town. Anyway the shift supervisors have to work with the personnel they are given. So they earn their pay, go through stress, and maybe pull their hair out. So anyway this new Homicide Detective is doing a follow-up on this victim at the county hospital. Doing his investigation. Later on the Detective advises his supervisor that he is at the county hospital checking on the victim, but renders no updates, stage of investigation, a lookout for the shooter nothing. Worse no information on the perpetrator, absolutely no update on the condition of the victim. The LT. said o.k. Is the victim low-sick or still living (DOA)? The detective answered on the radio, oh he's not sick, he's been shot. Lt. paused ok ..... I will meet you at the hospital.... hee, hee.

The first in a series of stories of police work. This portion is a light hearted. Maybe humorous inside look. Stories and humor in one. Read at your own risk. Don't tell anybody.

Captain Jim Stone is a Marine Corp War veteran. Served over forty-years of service with the Atlanta Police Dept and the Fulton County Police Dept. Has received many meritorious awards, and officer of the year awards. He is now retired, dealing in Real Estate, and as a hobby writing comedy books and songs. He writes under his character side kick Billy Bob "Junebug" Jonsun. But he is most proud of the privilege he had to serve in two great Departments in Atlanta, Georgia. He has a strong allegiance to those Departments, and the great people of Atlanta, Ga, but most of all to the men and women in blue and brown that it was an honor and privilege to serve with. Those people live in my heart forever. Their family.

16

TOW TRUCK

You have to have a sense of humor to do this job and keep your sanity. There was a saying that you don't have to be crazy to work here, but it helps. I know I used to tell a story about a bad accident. Most people want you to tell them a really funny incident, but even more want to hear the gory, brutal story of a bad wreck, shooting, or stabbing. like the news reports " If it bleeds, it leads" It's proved every time there is a bad accident the traffic slows down, backs up from people gawking, wanting to see all the gory scene. We call it rubbernecking. I never understood this action, maybe they want to relate what they saw and witnessed to their friends and family. So when people wanted to hear a really bloody story, maybe involving death, or the damage or loss of body limbs, anything messy. So when I got this question, I would relay a story of a multi-vehicle accident where there was a bunch of injuries such as torn off limbs and body parts. I was describing the accident, how it happened and the severe injuries to the drivers and passengers. After all the emergency equipment and wreckers had left the scene, I was walking the wreck scene looking for measurements and other evidence that may be on the scene and get ready to proceed to the hospital on a follow up. This particular time I was walking along the freeway emergency lane when I saw an object which turned out to be a big toe lost by one of the victims of the wreck. Now these body parts can be preserved, and can sometimes be reattached to the body. I could get an evidence bag and put the toe in it and take it to the hospital, maybe get some ice to help preserve it. Or I could call the ambulance back, but they need to continue on to the hospital for emergency medical care. The common question I was usually asked in a really concerned and troubled look: "What did you do?" I called for a Toe Truck.

17

ARMED ROBBERY

Another one I used to tell is that I responded to a hit and run call. A car side-swiped another car, scraping down the driver's side of both vehicles. Unfortunately, the victim of the side-swiped vehicle had his left arm and elbow hanging out the door with the door glass down. When the car side swiped the vehicle tore the driver's arm off, which stuck in the door as the car fled the scene. I was able to catch up with the hit and run vehicle and driver and recovered the arm. Normal question: "What did the guy say? Did he know about the arm stuck in his car door?" But most important is "What did you charge him with?" Social charges hit and run leaving the scene failing to maintain a lane and Arm Robbery.

18

J.R.

During your life, you meet a lot of different people from all walks of life. I like to call trails that we all travel down and we cross paths. I had an opportunity to cross a lot of paths of different people and animals. I found that I learned a lot about life, human nature from each one; rich, famous, and poor. Anyway, that's a different story I like to recall we are all squirrels looking for a nut.

Since I was a kid, I have been writing songs. As far back as 5 years old or younger. I used to entertain the family by request. They would tell me to get a broom, serving as a guitar, then I would do my rendition of Shotgun Boogie. It was rewarded by applause and laughter. I loved to write lyrics of songs and I listened to the radio as much as possible. I even did the Elvis twist before Elvis did (I was ahead of my time!). Then along came Johnny Cash and the Tennessee Two, Luther Perkins, and Marshall Grant. Though I was hooked on Rock n' Roll, and listened intently and was a fan. I was totally captured to the Johnny Cash sound; his voice, or more so, the music. Just the musical start of a song, the music told you who the artist was with J.R. So that is how it all started. I thought these guys were in a sample way, the best, Luther Perkins and Marshall Grant. I listened to all new releases.

This went on for years until I was in the Marines, where I kept up but found myself in many different war zones. Then I spent most of my time trying to stay alive. But long story short I made it through this season of my life and wound up in Atlanta, GA. All of a sudden, I was in the world of law enforcement. This is not another story but another book. Anyway, I started following Johnny Cash again more closely. I would find out when there was going to be a show and would get tickets early, and managed to get seats on the first or second row. This led to getting to meet Johnny Cash, along with members of the show. As a fan, I was really happy and pleased with getting to witness these performances and occasionally get to meet him and members of the show. I was really excited to witness the group live.

Then one day I had to appear in court. I was sitting outside the courtroom on a bench. Waiting to be called in as a witness to testify in a case. I was sitting on the bench with Officer Todd, just talking shop. I looked over at the next courtroom, and the bench outside where was one lone man sitting on the bench. Yes it was the man in black. I told Todd:

"That's Johnny Cash over there!"

Todd replied, "No that ain't Johnny Cash."

"Yes, it is too."

I got up and walked over to the next courtroom. For some reason, I was calm, not so overly excited. I had this feeling that I did not want to bother him, but I was just going to say hello to a good friend.

At the time, I did not really understand the gravity of the moment. Now I remember this meeting like it happened yesterday. I casually walked over to the bench. I noticed the hair combed back, and he was completely dressed in black. I was somewhat taken by surprise when I approached, as Mr. Cash stood up to greet me. He extended his hand for a strong handshake. I could not help but notice the rugged look, the deep voice. But I was really impressed by the large bone structure that fit tightly into a black coat with wide shoulders, large broad shoulders. I remember I asked if he was playing in town. If he was, I had missed getting tickets. He told me no, he was there to testify in a divorce proceeding of his brother. Then we had a short chat about his career, and some of his songs. Then he wrote me a short note and autograph on my court check. We had a one on one conversation for a minute. Then I was going to offer a witness room to get him out of the public view when people started showing up to get autographs. I think Todd spread the word in the courthouse. I really felt bad for my hero, who had apparently managed to sneak in to the courthouse unnoticed, testifying in a family divorce proceeding. I felt like my recognition, and telling Todd, who spread the word. But I did enjoy the heart to heart conversation, and realizing for a fact that this was a good man, with a down to earth honest attitude, with a good heart, who was courteous, a polite gentleman. I was very well pleased that the man offstage was probably equal to or greater than the performer onstage. It is really a great feeling to see into the heart of this man, and to realize that my following of the performer was real. I was also pleased that we parted ways as friends, John and Jim, which I will never forget. To put this in perspective, I have met political, Hollywood stars, local politicians and dignitaries,presidents, even Elvis and his shows. But I have to say this was the event of my life. I have often thought I wish that I could have spent more time, had more meetings, and attended more shows of (J.R.) Johnny Cash. Rest in peace, you made a difference on this earth and to one person, me, who will continue to write songs, stories, and poems. You were one of my great influences.

P.S. I found out through reading that Johnny Cash's parents could not settle or agree on a first name, so he was called J.R. 'Twas not until he went into the Air Force that he was required to have a first name, and John or Johnny was chosen. But he was born J.R. Cash (his dad was Ray Cash). Or he obtained his first name at Sun Records.

19

HEAD ON COLLISION

I served years as a field training officer. I would eventually get every new hire or rookie out of the academy. They would be assigned to a shift and a F.T.O. for a period of time. They would come and ride, drive in actual street patrol, on the job training that would cover actual patrol duties, calls for service, accident investigation, patrol techniques, and law enforcement. Also the steady patrol for criminals, such as drugs, thieves and burglars. A period of time to gain experience, advise, and to get acclimated to police work. I always tried to do the best job I could to teach these officers all I could to be well trained. I am glad that I did because there was a very good chance that I might well be working for them one day. But I did have one recruit come on the watch in the Field Training Program. This officer was well educated, neat and squared away in his uniform. He also had previous police experience with the Federal Government. This officer had a good personality, attitude, eager to learn, and was inquisitive. One thing I like about training in the field was it kept me up to date on all the laws, rules and regulations, patrol techniques, and constitutional updates. You never knew what you might have to deal with, and the issues and questions that covered a very broad area. But anyway this officer did a fine job in the program, and was assigned solo. He did request to be assigned to the morning watch 2300 hrs. to 0700 hrs. We called it the first shift (GRAVEYARD). A lot of the time this is third shift at a lot of places.

But this was the shift he wanted and he got it. This is a tough shift to work because it is just human nature, and normal to sleep at night. So the shift sometimes gets long, especially if activity and calls for service are slow. Even tho these guys are on solo you still try to assist them and check on them. Kind of take them under your wing to help them get acclimated to the job, and also back-up and safety factor.

One night I saw this officer's car parked in the parking lot of a well-known department store. I did notice that he had been parked there for some time. It was early morning, and very cold, in one of the winter months. I could see the exhaust and vapor from the tail pipe. Then I saw a tractor trailer pull right up in front of the police car, headlights to headlights. So I drove over to see what was up. This is what I found out and witnessed.

The trucker was looking for directions to a delivery address. He saw the officer's car parked and decided to ask him for directions. He pulled his truck right in front of the officer's car so the officer could clearly see the truck, and see him exit and approach his patrol car. The trucker pecked on the driver's side door glass. I seen the driver kind of take a quick step back from the patrol car. Evidently the officer's intentions were to park there for a few minutes to take a break or do a report. But he became warm and cozy. It was a quiet night not even a lot of radio traffic. So his eyes became heavy and he dozed off for a quick nap. I am sure, and later learned that the officer thought he had fell asleep driving, and was about to die in a head-on collision with a tractor-trailer.

But when the trucker pecked on the window, it startled the officer awake. the officer woke up facing the headlights and vision of a tractor-trailer coming right at him in a sure head-on collision. In fact he went into panic mode. He was terrified, face of fear, white in color. He tried to stop the car with a hard brake with his foot, almost standing on the brake, steering the steering wheel in a hard right defensive driving. Pure panic fashion, fighting fiercely to survive, facing certain death. Then he noticed there was no impact, no head-on with a tractor-trailer, no heart attack, no bad dream. It was back to reality. I had never seen anything like this incident. But to this relieved officer it had to be a terrifying learning experience that he will probably never forget. Life flashing before your eyes, facing death head-on. So a nervous wreck officer proud to be alive, saw the humor in it, and we went to get a calming cup of coffee. Later the officer left the department and went to a department in Washington, D.C.

A strange twist to this story, and to illustrate sometimes we live in a small world. My brother took his family to see Washington D.C., visit the sights a few years later. My nephew was twelve or thirteen years of age. Anyway while in D.C. my nephew meets a police officer, and they start talking. My nephew tells the police officer;

"My uncle is a policeman."

Oh really, where at?

He works in Atlanta.

I used to work in Atlanta. "What is his name? I may know him."

My nephew told him my name, and said you may not know him, they have a lot of officers work there. My nephew was surprised and shocked when the officer said, " Yes, I know him very well. He trained me."

It made my nephew's trip to Washington D.C. even greater because this officer took them under his wing, tour guide, and had long conversations with them that day. Small world, guess who it was? He told my family and nephew to be sure and tell him hello, and that he would always remember what he learned, and working with me and the experience. I hope he reads this because I want to thank him for his service, memories and his courtesy to my family, be safe brother. It was my honor and job and was a once in a lifetime experience and memory.

20

APRIL FOOLS

I recall that in the early days of my career. The Police Department started a squad called the stakeout squad. The squad worked a variety of crimes in high crime areas. One of the problems that they were assigned to and worked was armed robberies. A lot of these robberies occurred at a lot of convenience stores. These robberies at these convenient stores became very frequent and violent. In some of these robberies the clerks were abused, injured, and sometimes shot and some killed. The perpetrator(s) would usually at the least beat the clerk, clean out the cash drawer, and sometimes the safe. These robberies did occur at different locations, and times of the day. A majority of them occurred at night, or early in the morning hours. It became a serious epidemic problem. It was such a frequent occurrence that it was took for granted. The stores became known as the stop n rob. It became a very dangerous job to work for the public. In fact it was getting hard to find people to work this high risk job. Some of the stores started closing at night. So then they started breaking in, but at least no one was injured or killed.

So the stake-out squad got assigned to different convenience stores to combat the robberies. It was a team, usually two partners staked-out inside a store, and the rest of the squad monitoring along with patrol units and other police personnel. All ready to respond as back-up. The squad was successful with apprehensions with these tactics. The result was arrests, robberies cleared, and decreased robbery attempts. There were several shooting incidents where the perpetrators were violent and resisted. Sometimes they were just dangerous or strung out on drugs, and armed.

These were armed and dangerous criminals that want that money, and will do anything to get it, beat the clerk, shoot customers. Anything.

I was in the court one early morning seated in the court room waiting for my cases to be called. Basically this is a court session that hears violations of city ordinances, probable cause hearing for criminal cases for state criminal court, and felony cases for the Grand Jury and Superior Court. So while you wait you listen to the other cases presented. I could not help but notice in the jail prisoner seats a prisoner seated that was heavily bandaged in white bandages. A black male in his twenties, medium height and build that looked ill and it appeared he just got out of the hospital. I was curious as to what is his story, and what happened to this guy. I know he is seated in the prisoners incarcerated guarded section. He had also received a severe injury.

Finally the prisoner's name was called, and he managed to hobble up to in front of the bench to face the judge. This list of charges was read off. You are charged with armed robbery, aggravated assault on a police officer, firearm violation, etc. How do you plead? The guy entered a plea of not guilty. Apparently he is not new to the system.

One of the officers from the stake-out squad was in court to testify to evidence and facts in this case, and to identify the person in court that committed these crimes. Judge said ok officer, what are the facts in the case. What happen? The officer started out by stating the crimes charged occurred in this jurisdiction and venue. He stated that he was assigned to a certain convenience store that had experienced robberies in the past. The officer went into a short story on how he was a member of the stake-out squad. How the squad, due to a rash of robberies had been assigned to this particular date and time. He was assigned to this particular store as a team with his partner. He said they entered the store, explained the procedure to the clerk, and explained instructions. The officer described briefly how the squad operated by positioning themselves in the back room, storage room, office and look through a glass or camera, where they had a clear view of the clerk, the front door, counter, and interior of the store, through that glass, mirror, and video screens. They took such a position on this occasion.

In the early morning hours two black males entered the store dressed in dark clothing and wearing knit skull caps. One went to the counter immediately, one stayed closer to the front door to watch the lot and front door. They both pulled hand guns and pointed them at the clerk "Ok mother-fucka this is a robbery. Open the drawer, give me all the money, put it in a bag.

Hurry, I'll blow your fuckin head off. Move, Hurry up! We're going to kill your ass if you don't hurry!"

The officer testified the team saw and heard all this violent dangerous situation. An armed robbery in progress. They heard the demands, violence and seen guns in the perpetrators hands. They were armed and dangerous. The officer stated the officers stepped out of the backroom, with guns drawn in a cover situation, dressed in blue identifiable police uniform, with a badge. The officer testified that both officers called out, Police, Police Officers, freeze, drop you weapons. You are under arrest. Do it now. Both gunmen turn their guns towards the officers and shots were exchanged. One of the perpetrators was shot right in front of the counter and register. The other one was shot at the store front door as he tried a shoot and escape. This is the person in court, because he was sent to the hospital with gunshot wounds. Because the other perp was killed at the scene. The officer identified the guy in court as the perpetrator shot at the front of the store and hospitalized. Hearing set for today after dismissal from the hospital.

The judge said ok sir, would you like to make a statement on the officer's testimony?

Well uh ye know ye honor. We did go in the store early morning like the officer say, but we didn't know who they was. They came out of the backroom with guns pointed at us, and say April Fools mother-fucker and started shooting at us. We had guns wiff us and we tried to defend ourselves. The judge bound it over to the Grand Jury.

Work in to Fill Space

The thoughts in my heart and head. I know that like everyone else my blood is red. But what I think is dropping on paper in ink.

Still bravely facing the struggles of life facing all the challenges of an Evil world.

I didn't do everything right.
But I didn't do anything wrong,
I can sleep at night.

21

AN HONEST CRIMINAL

When I was a rookie they may put me in a Paddy Wagon, patrol car, in all parts of the city. Sometimes I had to go to what they called a foot beat or a special assignment at a specific location. I was what you call a roustabout. It wasn't bad, you got to work different beats, with different duties and crime problems. It was also a great opportunity to learn the city, and gain valuable experience. I cannot over emphasize the importance of experience, and the ability to think logically, take time and be cautious. Do not over react. Keep learning. Back in the day you were basically on your own, no guidance. You learned by experience, trial and error mistakes, and mistakes of others. It was really a challenge. In later years I was one of the first officers in the Field Training Officer Program. Where you train in the field with the F.T.O. for months before you are solo. Good program. I did not have this luxury when I came on the job.

I don't know whether I was a good observant police officer, or I just had a knack for falling into a pile my whole career. I don't think it was luck, it may be luck that I have survived. I know a lot of things just don't look right to me, and it turns out it was not right. It was criminal. It is a sense or trait I could never teach. I will always remember a judge was telling a defense counsel about my observation of his client. Why I looked at his client from the start.

The Judge stated to counsel that this officer had a reasonable suspicion, then probable cause that a crime was being committed, and one was committed. He also has a sense and knowledge that something didn't look right. I don't know how he knows it. It's a sense, expertise, and his job to know. I can't explain it. I know horse people who can just look at different horses and be able to tell a good horse and capabilities just by looking. They just know. He gave more examples, and how the. observations turn out to be true. But I will never forget the judge's explanation of what I was about. I never could explain it to anyone. He is a police officer, and it is his job to know. It's also a trust. This judge will always remain in my memory forever. He was truly a very wise man, and even a greater judge.

I always tried to be nice and polite to people and respect them as human beings, creations of God. But unfortunately some people won't let you be nice. All they see is a uniform. I always wanted them to know why I stopped them, or why I was checking them for violations of the Law. I also wanted to make sure they were advised of their rights and all charges. I tried not to brow beat, coerce or threaten them. I don't even like being put under pressure or duress. It is not personal. It is my job. It is different with criminals. They are street smart, and know how to play the system, and the officer.

One night I got assigned a beat car in the down town area. I observed a vehicle, a sedan travelling south through town, in an erratic manner, weaving in and out of the lane but slow. The driver was a white male seem to be preoccupied with the steering column or equipment. The vehicle had a tail light out. I stopped the vehicle, told the driver why I stopped him. I asked for his driver's license, registration, insurance information. Which he could not produce any of. I checked the tag for stolen (VIN) and registration. No stolen but the names didn't match the driver. The driver was placed under arrest for violations. I advise him of his rights. He was searched for weapons, and placed in the back seat. I called for a wrecker to impound the car. I got in my patrol car to do my paper work and wait on the wrecker. My prisoner was really starting to act real nervous now. So I thought I would try a little humor to lighten the situation. "So I said, Ok where did you steal this car?" He stated, up at the Gas Light Company, sir. So I called radio back and told them to run that tag and VIN again. I have information that it is stolen. Radio advised yes it is stolen. It was stolen about twenty minutes ago at the Gas Light Company. Before I could get the tickets wrote and the report started several cars responded to my location especially Auto Theft Detectives. Who wanted my prisoner and the collar. But I was a rookie, and I did not fully understand the process, or how the system works. But in that day Detectives worked shifts, and would do follow-up investigations, arrest and handle court.

Then I went to where most cases the officer had to handle everything all the way through. It turned from fun and excitement to a challenge and police work. Good experience though.

22

GET A MOTEL ROOM

Well, a motel franchise was having a serious problem with a cat burglar jimmying the locks on guest's rooms, entering and stealing wallets, purses, jewelry, cash, anything left out while the guests slept in the bed. Crazy stuff, almost unbelievable. There was also the thought that guests might be making this up for insurance claims. So this was finally discounted after so many guests reported thefts with that old saying, "We've been robbed." I saw this scene played out in a movie. Planes, Trains, and Automobiles. In the movie, Steve Martin and John Candy were staying in a motel room. A cat burglar entered the room while they slept. The theft was not discovered until the next day, when they were eating breakfast and discovered all their money was gone. In fact, they accused each other. Then that famous term by John Candy, 'We've been robbed,' and Steve Martin replying, 'You think so? Memories of this cat burglar come back, same situation. So the investigation starts, What the hell is going on? Who is it? Employee? Employee, helping a perpetrator with key, credit card, or burglary tool? There was no sign of forcible entry. How was the bolt lock opened? Need a key? We had to find out because we had a lot of victims. Management was worried and really scared and they had no answers or solutions to the problem. So what do you do? Call the police or talk to an officer friend and beat officer you know for help and a solution. This is where I was instantly involved in the investigation and solution to the question. "Where do you start?" I started out by telling the manager and her employees to pay special attention to the locks, make sure no keys were out. Examine the door locks carefully when the room was rented or someone checked out. I did this to indicate we wanted to solve the theft, and it was a positive action to indicate we were working on the case. But to my surprise, this turned out to be a good move. I was informed by the manager that they had just checked out a guest in one particular room. The basement room was on a floor rooms had been burglarized. They wanted to know if I could come by, and check the rooms, doors and windows. We checked the whole room and ask if any keys were out. The answer was no. Then we were checking the room front door. It was discovered that the bolt lock would not fully engage and click, but appeared lock. I checked the bolt lock and then the bolt lock hole, and discovered up in the hole was a piece of white paper, like a piece of folded paper or a napkin. I tried the bolt lock which seemed to engage, but a closer look and try of the lock indicated that the bolt lock appeared locked but was loose and not locked. No click, the paper held it unlocked. So I knew whoever rented this room could be the next victim. It was set up for entry. Now it was time to set up stage two of our plan, to solve the burglaries and apprehend the perpetrator. I would become more involved in this crime investigation.

So my plan went like this. We would show the room rented and occupied by a potential victim. The manager would be in a room across the hall observing the room and call us if she saw anybody enter. Then I decided it may be more beneficial to do a stake-out inside the room to catch and arrest the perp. But be careful what you ask for. I was nominated to perform this duty. So what happened was we left the door as-is the manager would be in the room across the hall which turned out to be a beneficial plan. I would be inside the room as the guest. It was a gamble, but this appeared to be the mode of operation for the perp and was our best chance to catch the perp. Maybe we would get lucky, maybe. So I come on shift, went and got me some coffee and some snacks. I had my walkie-talkie to stay in touch with the other officers. I checked in with the manager who was across the hall. Then I proceeded to my room for a long night. My first concern was the noise of the walkie-talkie, I had to keep it all the way down due to the voice traffic of the beat cops. I covered it with a pillow to make sure. I did have the room phone where I checked in periodically with the precinct and supervisor. So I settled in for a long night and hopefully a fulfilling arrest of a dangerous criminal and clearing up a bunch of burglaries. But it was quite tedious, nerve racking. Where is the best place to be in the room? How and when and where will I take him down? What if he is armed? One question after another. Is this the right plan? Are we sure this is the set up? Is this the next victim's room? What if there is more than one perp? Anyway, I'm here, deal with it and hope for the best and depend on quick backup response. Was I nervous, uptight anxious, apprehensive? Absolutely. But I was also young and dumb and had no fear. Always wanted to be in the action, and loved to arrest hardened criminals and get them off the streets. So I am in my room waiting. I went in the room about 2330 hours or 11:30 p.m. We had no idea when these perps were breaking in. But looking back on it now, I should have known that it would be early morning hours when the perp would know that the victim had the lights out, clothes and valuables on the dresser. Room quiet, guest sound asleep. But you can never be sure.

But the stake-out went something like this. So I had the door to watch, using the peephole for a view of the hall. Then I had the room windows with the curtains drawn. I had to worry about entry through the window, but that would be very hard and noisy. Was I a silhouette through the curtain? So I turned the lights off to make sure, and I did not move around much. Be patient, do not blow my cover, be ready at any time. The room had two beds. I sat on both, alternating my position where I would have the best view of the room, cover in case of a shootout and where I would have the best element of surprise and advantage. I placed some items on the dresser and made the bed look like someone was in it asleep with pillows. Looked good. The minutes drag by to an hour, no activity. Then to the hours, many trips to the door peephole to look, one bed to the other even into the bathroom to break the monotony. The hours drug by up to maybe 0300 hours in the morning. I checked with the supervisor several times on the phone reporting nothing yet. So the hours slowly ticked away. It's probably 0400 hours. I've checked the peephole at least a hundred times, now my walkie-talkie is dead after being on all night. I called the supervisor and told him I had no communication because my radio battery was dead. So I also notified the manager across the hall my radio was out, so stand by her phone in case I need backup, because I may not be able to get to a phone. So the supervisor said maybe we should pull off and try it again tonight. It is getting about 0430 hours now. I told him I would give it a while longer because I believe this is our last chance. So I moved around the room for a while, sat on both beds, went in the bathroom and I thought well maybe this is a dry run, and I figured it wrong. But I had this gut feeling, and this situation did not look right. So after a few more minutes, almost 0450 hours no radio, no activity, maybe it's just not my day. So I get everything together. I go into the bathroom leave the bathroom with the light on and open the door. I go to the room door and grab the door knob to leave. Well, I looked through the peephole and see one of the biggest eyeballs trying to look through the hole from the other side. This is it! I hear jiggling of the locks and the door knob starts to turn and I lightly let my hand turn with the knob and as the door starts to open I backed up into the bathroom and thank God I left the bathroom door open. It saved my bacon because if I had been heard or detected the perp could easily run. So I kept backing up until I saw a large black male about 6'3",

230 lbs with a small screwdriver in his hand. He was in his early 30s. I let him come all the way in the room. I pulled my service revolver, I said

Halt, police! You are under arrest!

I pointed my gun right at his head, he had moved to the hall in what I thought was an attempt to escape. I told him to drop the screwdriver, which he did. Then I told him to put his hands on his head, cross his legs and drop to his knees. He hesitated like he might resist or run, I shouted

Don't make me shoot you. If you move a hair, I'm going to shoot.

"You need to get my partner; he is just down the hall behind you."

I still had my back in the door of my room. I kicked on the wall for the manager., I heard her say

I heard it all and they are on their way

I knew he was trying to divert my attention long enough to run. He knew he was close to the push bar exit door near this room. This was preplanned in case he was detected and had to flee, he could be gone in seconds. I did not believe he had a partner or an accomplice somewhere behind me in the hall. I had already planned for two people and did not dismiss that possibility, so I put my back to the wall so I could swivel around in any direction. I could get off shots to both perpetrators in a second if I needed to. This was my next course of action. It was heavy stress one of those butt puckers. Is he going to attack? Are more perps going to attack? Will I have to use deadly force to protect myself? It seemed like forever for backup to arrive.

A few minutes later one officer arrived and came to the back main door which was locked. The perp kept trying to divert my attention. I finally told him to shut up and that if he moved I was going to start shooting his body parts. He finally shut up and I got other officers on the scene. I was glad to see the back up officers, and that I did not have to take action that would injure or kill anyone. I know I was in a precarious situation. I could tell this criminal would not hesitate to hurt or kill me with opportunity. Thank God for looking over me. But it was a lonely feeling. The perp was read his rights, advised of charges, and transported to the county jail with several burglary charges. The subject had a long rap sheet for thefts, burglary, escape, assault on a police officer, and aggravated assault. He was bound over to the grand jury in his preliminary hearing. The investigation was turned over to detectives who made additional burglary charges at the motel, and he was connected to at last count close to 200 burglaries at different motels and jurisdictions, most along the freeways I-75 and I-285. Still counting, but I was proud of my one case and the perpetrator in jail. Very happy police administration and a whole lot of motel employees.

23

YOU RECKON YOU COULD LET ME OFF AT THE NEXT EXIT?

I used to work what was called an extra job at a popular Sports bar. Working security, front door and maintaining peace and order. I also had to make bank drops with the manager. The bar was open to the early morning hours, It was a good place to work because, business people, politicians, actors, celebrity sports figures were always coming by. It was also frequented by members of local sport teams and owners. It is part of the job to get to know these people, and all the managers and employees of the bar, bus boy, waitresses, band members and regular customers.

I did become acquainted with a young man, working as a bus boy. He was the typical young early twenties guy, slender with long brown hair. Real friendly with a good personality that was a steady worker, and done his job well. He was a student working his way through school. We had many conversations, and we became pretty good friends. I will call him Jeff. The names have been changed to protect the innocent. I know that after the bar closed and all the work was done the crew would have some shift drinks, play pool, listen to music and talk. Sometimes for quite a while. Jeff participated.

One morning I was working patrol on the morning watch (2300--0700 hrs). It was after 0400 hrs. I received a call to the freeway. A main entrance ramp to the freeway. It was a reported accident of a motorcycle vs. tractor trailer. There was also an ambulance and fire and rescue on the way for possible serious injury or a fatality. When I arrived on the scene I could only find a damaged motorcycle. No driver to be found. I checked, along with fire and rescue, the entire area, lanes, the median, side of the roadway, in the grass, nothing. I got the motorcycle out of the roadway before it caused another accident. I continued to investigate and talk to any witnesses. Witnesses stated that all they saw was a motorcycle travel down the entrance ramp at a high rate of speed, enter the freeway, and evidently did not see the tractor-trailer traveling in the lane. The motorcycle collided with the trailer whirling it in the air. But no one saw the driver thrown in the air or land anywhere. The witnesses stated the tractor-trailer continued on East. I put a lookout on the truck with the best description and information I had. I checked everywhere, ramps, lanes, grass. No driver, no debris, no blood? Then I put a lookout for all tractors to be stopped and checked. This time of morning there was not that many, but it would require help from other jurisdictions. So I started driving East to see if I could locate the truck. I was thinking that the motorcycle driver could be hung underneath the trailer or in the wheels and thrown off in a lane somewhere. I was pretty sure that the driver of the tractor-trailer was probably not aware of the situation or that an accident occurred. I was checking to see if the motorcycle driver had been drug down the freeway? A lot of bad scenarios.

Then I started getting calls that motorist were seeing a tractor-trailer East on the freeway, and a male was hanging onto the trailer, and dangling in the air from the rear of the trailer. I speeded up to get down to where these incidents were being reported, some fifteen miles. I arrived in the area with officers from other jurisdictions. I seen a male on the back of a trailer like flying in the air like one of them football team flags on cars and trucks. With the help of other officers with blue lights and sirens we got the truck stopped. I got the male off the trailer, but he still really didn't want to turn loose. He was clawed like a spider, and kept that clawed position even after we got him off the trailer, locked in claws. He looked like a terrified spider in position. Wow! This was really a butt-puckering experience. I guess sometimes you don't know your own strength. When supernatural strength takes over, or is divine intervention? It sure was an amazing sight to see, scary for all. Dangling, hanging on for dear life for fifteen miles in the back-lash wind of the truck. Amazingly and not injured, but really shook up, survived the wind.

The guy was really glad to see me, glad that I got the truck stopped and got him off the trailer. He said he had almost gave up hope that he would survive. He was full of thanks, and gratitude, even gave me a great big hug, said I saved his life. The young man was lucky, not injured, scared, but happy to be alive. But extra happy to see me, because it was the bus boy Jeff, my friend from my extra job.

The truck driver was in total shock, and was totally unaware of anything that happened or the situation. And for sure did not know he had a passenger hanging on the back of his trailer. All the what ifs.

But it was time to do the paperwork and then get ready for the next call. But this is a famous story and was talked about for months and probably still brought up nowadays.

24

MR. GOODWRENCH?

Some things you just can't teach. Sometimes I believe you develop a sixth sense. No reasoning, but just a sense that this just doesn't look right. I don't believe it's psychic, but it is close. Kind of a mystery. I have heard it referred to as lucky, rather than good police work. In police work, you can do a hundred good things, but you will be remembered by the one bad decision for the rest of your career. It's a tough business, lots of competition, jealousy, and ego wars. Then the factor of politics, and the buddy system. I just come to work to do my job to protect and serve. I wanted to get criminals off the streets. One incident that occurred one hot summer day in July, I think. I was sitting driver window to driver window, side by side in a popular department store parking lot, with my beat partner. Located on a heavily traveled five lane highway. I noticed like a large sedan traveling south, the window was down, and the driver had on a winter coat? Then I noticed that the vehicle was traveling quite fast and, was weaving? The driver seemed to be preoccupied and not concentrating on driving. I remember I told my beat partner.

"Come on. This guy just don't look right."

So here we go southbound in pursuit to catch up with this vehicle. The vehicle seemed to keep operating erratically, failing to maintain a lane, then the vehicle made a sudden right turn onto a side road. So it was time to blue light and make a traffic stop to see what the driver's problem was. After the stop, and asking for a driver's license, proof of insurance. It did not take long to see signs of a real problem. The driver had on a full length trench coat on a very hot 90 degree July day. I could see his pants were wet on the knees, his speech was slurred, eyes were red. I did notice that he had an odor of some type of alcoholic beverage. So this led to a possibility of driving under the influence of drugs or alcohol. My partner was going to administer a few field sobriety evaluations, but he was patting this guy down for weapons for safety purposes, then it was discovered besides the trench coat and wet knees, the back of his pants were cut out all the way to the front, only the belt area and pants leg left.

Back in the day I had a similar incident. So I started comparing. I had an exhibitionist who would go to where the ladies gathered. One place was where women played tennis, same mode, he would wear a trench coat. After a few minutes he would open the coat, expose his nude body underneath. When I finally caught the guy in the act. He had a trench coat on, he had sowed pant legs to the bottom of the coat, and it appeared that he had pants on. Under the coat he was nude. He would open his coat and exposed himself.

Then I heard my partner in a loud shocked voice after the cut away pants were discovered, and he was checking for weapons. Then I heard my partner discovered something and was asking questions in an excited, surprised, startled manner shocked. I responded quickly because I thought the guy had a concealed weapon.

The jail personnel like to find weapons so they can blame the officer for a poor search and of course it hits the news media and your Department Heads.

"What is that between your legs? Is that a wrench?"

"Yeah, a wrench."

"Is it inserted in your ass?"

"Yeah I am weird."

Well, this opened up a new can of worms and changed the investigation. First, I now knew why the subject could not walk straight. Now, it is for sure that he would have to go to the hospital if he was charged. I asked him if he was alright, or if he needed medical attention. I knew that the jail intake would not accept a prisoner with a wrench up his ass. I notified a supervisor of the situation, and his advice was just don't pull it out, which was my very last option. So I issued tickets for the traffic violations. He did not appear to be intoxicated enough that he was an unsafe driver. So the cases were set for my next court date. To say the least, this case traveled around the department and to all adjacent agencies, maybe state or nation. It became known as "Mr. Goodwrench" case. Not to my surprise, when I came back to work my next shift, usually when you came to work you check your box, they call it a pigeon hole, a box where you receive lookouts, tag checks, messages, reports, subpoena, etc. Anyway, when I check my box, there was a large Craftsman adjustable wrench!! It was the talk of the police dept. and not to mention police community and would have been more so if he had been incarcerated at the jail. But this was not a concealed weapon, besides he would have to go to the hospital first to remove it. So that led up to the court date where the subject would appear on his charges. The court date came up.

Well I finished my shift and then went to court. A crowd of people were standing outside the courtroom. Inside, every bench was full, and we had people standing around the walls, standing room only. But this turned out to be an uneventful appearance. When the defendant's name was called, and a plea entered for his violations, he pleaded that he was guilty as charged and did not want to make a statement or explanation. This was a disappointment to the audience, and even court personnel who wanted to hear all the gory or funny testimony, facts and evidence in this case, and it had spread all over.

To illustrate the reputation of this case, not too long ago I think it was in Florida, a prisoner was admitted to the jail, and had a pistol concealed up his ass. It was national news. But I heard from different officers from all over, even the FBI that the 'Mr. Goodwrench' case had been topped. Like I have said before, every time you think you have seen everything, something weirder happens. Some consolation is that we found this on the scene and nobody was transported to the jail, which could have been a tragedy if it had been a concealed weapon and not found before transport.

Because bringing a prisoner into the jail with a weapon is a poor prisoner search and a critical safety factor for everyone. Make good searches. I have found weapons, money, and drugs hidden in the crevices. This is my first wrench. I named it the "Mr. Goodwrench" case.

25

OLD SCHOOL

It's hard to put into words and say what Old School means. Personally, it involves the color "Blue." It's hard to get a true definition it seems.

Everybody seems to know who they are, but to describe one they don't know what to say. Let's start, I guess with all the clichés. He says what he means, and means what he says. He believes in the Golden Rule. "Do unto others as you would have them do unto you." But, he keeps in mind "Do unto others before they do it to you." Bend, but don't break the rule. In his mind your word and a handshake should do.

Sometimes the label "Pig" comes to mind. A better word to define would be hard to find. Pride, integrity and guts, that describes him pretty much. Don't play him as a fool, that's another rule. Don't touch me, and I won't touch you. This is not only physical, but also mental respect. Both are insults to him personally, and his intellect. He works hard to try to stay politically correct.

C.Y.A. Cover your ass is the Rule of the Day: But Murphy's Law always gets in the way. I've asked, "what is Old School" from friends of mine. It really can't be defined, but character and demeanor come to mind. You will know one, when you see one, in many, but substantial ways. I would say first, his hair is receding and is different shades of gray. The days have passed, and he has aged: The volumes of experience and knowledge you can see by the texture and lines in his face.

His eyes have a thousand-mile stare. Calculating and shrewd, you know he is going to think every option through. When he has all the facts, and something he can prove. Then make a decision, but he will figure out what to do. To protect and serve is the guiding rule. The knowledge, experience and abilities he has, they don't teach in school.

Forget the bullshit stories. He's heard them all many times before. Cut to the chase, and tell the truth. What's right or wrong, what's black or white. Is the easiest way. He wants to stay out of the area that is gray. You can almost see the wheels turn in his head. It's like he suddenly sees the light. Let's get it right so we can all sleep tonight.

He is a thin line between good and evil. But he takes time to listen, gives and expects respect, and hasn't give up on people yet. He is a dying breed; he is an endangered species. The likes of which, again, we will never see. He is truly a treasure our society needs.

He does things the old fashioned way, not perfect, but close to the right way. His personal thoughts are sometimes kept silent, and he'll never say; he wants it that way. But all of them love to tell stories, and reflect on memories of the good ole days. How they know things, I can't say. That just don't sound right, that just don't look right, a sixth sense comes into play.

Well, look at all the time I've spent, trying to define and describe something that is infinite. Old School, you just know.

But now you have some idea when you hear it said, or see one on the job. When you do, you know. He hangs his laundry, life and reputation on the line everyday. His debt and dues to society have been paid. He has done it for years and years. Why? Because he was built that way. He's Old School. "Blessed are the peacemakers, for they shall see heaven."

Partners:
Jean Stone
2010

By: Captain James (Jim) Allen Stone
aka: billy bob "Junebug" Jonsun
2006©

Printed in the United States
By Bookmasters